D0459544

To Dick &Lynn,
A reminder of many
Pleasant evenings!

Cheers
Michael & Sue
June '87

THE ENGLISH PUB

# The ENGLISH PUB

## Andy Whipple & Rob Anderson

· *with 185 colour illustrations* ·

Thames and Hudson

First published in Great Britain in 1985 by Thames and Hudson Ltd, London

Produced by Howard Jacobsen, Triad, Fairfax, California

Designed by Rob Anderson

Photographs by Andy Whipple

Printed and bound in Japan by Dai Nippon Printing Co., Ltd.

*To Frederick George Biles, with admiration for his genius; and to Jesse, Berend, and Remko with faith in theirs*

# CONTENTS

Acknowledgment, warmly: Emily Emerson for tolerance
and an eye for the dangling modifier, Rose Loeff for patience,
Naomi Barry for wings, Danny Blythe, Vickie Cherry, Leigh Dean,
Fred Durant, Simon and Caroline Earl, Anne-Elise and Van
Fleisher, Brian Glover, David Hall, Fred Hill, Somerset Moore,
Michael Parsons, Alan Perry, Norman Rushton, Tony Saint, Val
and Keith Wells-West for help and enthusiasm, Richard Boston for
inspiration, Sheila at Kodak in Hemel Hempstead for watching over
our film, Bill Anderson for pointing out the first pub sign, and
Elizabeth Whipple

# HISTORY & TRADITIONS

Any history of pubs and the art of brewing must begin with the broader story of English hospitality. The pub, which historian Richard Keverne declared to be "the healthiest, most human, and most characteristic of English institutions," began not as a commercial venture, but as an extension of the private home. The story involves everything from chemistry to politics, but the central element has always been people. As Thomas Burke says in his slim but wonderful book *English Inns*, "The most important feature of an inn— more important than age, architectural grace, oak beams, its yard, or even its kitchen—is the landlord."

Although much of their history is shared, pubs and inns have gone separate ways. The coaching inn of old has become the modern hotel, and the alehouse, the pub. For some time, both were required by law to provide lodging. Today, many pubs still offer rooms for the night or Bed and Breakfast, and most hotels have a bar where drinks are served, though neither is required legally to do so. The term *inn* has come to be used for both, often causing confusion for today's traveler. The original distinction remains, however, in the atmosphere. The inn-hotel developed out of a traveler's need for safe lodging, and the alehouse-pub from a community's desire for drink and socializing.

Hundreds of years ago, beer was a domestically produced com-

modity, like bread or clothing. When the brewer of an especially good beer became known by word of mouth, he or she could expect visitors. If a home-brewed beer drew a sufficiently large and steady crowd, the brewer's home would become something of a meeting place, or "public house." These first pubs, also known as alehouses, soon emerged as contenders with the local churches as centers of cultural activity. Weddings, births and deaths, political transactions, and payment of wages were all invariably celebrated with one or more pints of ale. When demand for a certain beer reached the point where the brewer sold or transported it to other homes, the

alehouse was often transformed into a full-time brewery.

Commercial drinking establishments are recorded as early as 745, when the Archbishop of York decreed that "priests are not to eat or drink in taverns." Long before trains and automobiles revolutionized the handling and distribution of such perishables as beer, England was dotted with tiny breweries, each serving customers within the range of a horse-drawn wagon on a primitive road—a radius of perhaps five to ten miles. The beer was put up in wooden barrels, and

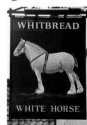

all breweries employed at least one full-time cooper—a craftsman skilled in fitting oak staves,

*Seventeenth-century coaching scene, from a sign painted by George Biles.*

hoops, and bungs to make leakproof containers.

Today, a handful of breweries still use horse-and-wagon transport. The practice is justified as being more economical than trucking within very short distances. And the public relations aspects are obvious. The wooden barrels have been largely replaced by metal ones (clearly lighter and easier to clean, though experts disagree about differences in flavor), but wood is still used occasionally. And cooperage, though an endangered craft, persists.

The proliferation of inns and pubs resulted not only from brewing skill but from gradual advances in transportation. At first, people traveled only out of

spiritual or business necessity. In the fourteenth century, inns offered extremely basic accommodation. Guests might find a pint of ale and lodging for the night, but usually were obliged to bring along their own food.

Both the range of travel and the

*The cooper is an increasingly rare craftsman. Seamless machine-made metal barrels have almost completely replaced hand-fitted wooden casks.*

numbers of travelers increased in the fifteenth century. More inns and pubs were built, with facilities gradually improving. By the sixteenth century carpets had been introduced, and the better rooms had tapestries and other decorations on the walls.

In 1552, during the reign of Edward VI, Parliament passed an act requiring the licensing of "tippling houses." Prior to this time, the magistrates had had power only to suppress and punish troublesome pubs and publicans; this act gave them the power to *select*, thus elevating the alehouse keeper to a position of privileged citizen. Also at this time, guidelines were established to control volume of drinking and to require alehouses to provide accommodations and "wholesome victuals to all such as honest occasions shall repair to their house."

The seventeenth century was the age of the coach, immortalized fondly in contemporary "Coach and Horses" signs. Many of what Burke calls "today's historic treasures"—

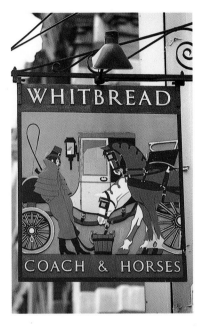

elegant old inns, like the Cotswold stone George and Pilgrims in Glastonbury—were built in this era. The tradition of English hospitality had established itself.

Home brewing dominated until the seventeenth century. Samuel Pepys, in his mid-seventeenth-century *Diaries*, makes more than one mention of stopping to enjoy a particular ale made by John Bide, then a sheriff of London. In the towns, however, innkeepers started their own breweries, and some individuals were employed as professionals, earning their livelihoods solely from making beer.

Inns and pubs continued their growth in the next century. This period saw the founding of England's great breweries, whose forces would eventually become the major influence on the nature of the pub. London, of course, was the center of activity: Whitbread was established here in 1742, Charrington in 1776, and Courage in 1789. In the town of Burton (famous for its water), Worthington was started in 1744, followed by Bass in 1777. In Ireland, Arthur Guinness opened his doors in 1759.

In 1760, five London breweries each produced fifty thousand barrels (a barrel is thirty-six gallons), a large output even today. Twenty years later, six breweries each were producing eighty thousand barrels annually. Enormous fortunes were made, thanks to advances in brewing technique. The developing science of chemistry, for example, made possible mineral identification in regional water supplies, thus permitting the brewing of Burton ales in London and London stouts in Burton. Temperature control led to

year-round brewing. The large city breweries were able to produce consistently high-quality products and to price them competitively. In the country, home-

brew pubs and small breweries fell behind technologically, still using trial-and error methods to make beers of erratic quality.

In the late eighteenth and nineteenth centuries, the days of the Industrial Revolution, all of England grew and prospered. In this period the *tied house* system emerged. For simple economic reasons, breweries bought, sometimes after a period of leasing, as many individual pubs in their areas as they could. The benefits were obvious: control of the retail outlet as well as the means of production. In modern business jargon this practice is called vertical integration. Some might call it monopoly. In England, however, it became, and remains, the accepted prac-

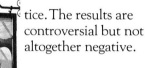

tice. The results are controversial but not altogether negative.

Today, more than eighty-five percent of England's seventy-thousand pubs are tied houses—owned outright by the breweries. Publicans in tied houses are called *tenants* if they share in the financial success of the pubs, and *managers* if they handle daily operations for a salary. A pub owned by a private individual is called a *free house*, and these words usually appear on the pub sign. For new tenants, a probationary year is part of the first lease. Waiting lists are common. Tenants pay rent to the brewery, usually provide their own fixtures, and are required to sell only the parent brewery's beer. The number of tied houses owned by a single

brewery ranges from one (home-brew pubs) to the almost unbelievable figure of ninety-eight hundred (owned by Bass, the largest brewer in Europe). A publican-owned free house is "free" to purchase beer from any brewery it chooses.

The Industrial Revolution created wealth and mobility on almost every level of society,

although not to the immediate benefit of existing inns and pubs. Emerging quickly as both fact and symbol of Britain's strength, the newly developed rail network had a brief but for a time crippling effect. Transportation routes, many of them centuries old, were abandoned, essentially overnight. Formerly busy public houses fell on hard times. In the eloquent lament of Burke, "the bustle was stilled . . . the bright lights extinguished, and the warm rooms empty, occupied only by the chill." Today, numerous pubs hang the sign Railway Inn. The majority of these were built very quickly, near passenger stations, in response to the demands of a new style of travel. It took the development of motorized vehicles to revitalize the remaining public houses.

"When the first English road was made," says Burke, "the first English public house was born. 600 years separate today's roadhouse from Chaucer's Tabard. Yet the atmosphere and tradition are one. Only the appointments are different. Each is typical of its period. They and their company are linked in an unbroken line."

# How Beer Is Made

The terms *ale* and *beer* are often used interchangeably, even by experts; sometimes writers will distinguish between the two but fail to agree on which is which. In this book, real English beer (whether identified as "real ale" or "traditional beer") is considered to be *ale*, a subclass of the broader category *beer*. Ale—a family including stout, bitter, mild, pale ale, light ale, old ale, and the potent, seasonally brewed "winter warmer"—is distinct from other beers in three important ways.

First, ale uses a top-fermenting strain of yeast. Beer (Continental- and American-style) uses a bottom-fermenting variety; these types are most accurately called lagers, from a German word meaning "store," because part of their production in-

volves storing, or lagering, in refrigerated tanks.

Second, ale has more hops than beer. Hops, introduced in the fifteenth-century, give the drink its characteristic flavor and one of its nicknames, "bitter." Hops also act as a preservative—ale and beer having predated refrigerators by hundreds of years.

As any Englishman will tell

you, a good beer shows its subtle flavors when it is not ice cold. Finally, then, and perhaps most important, ale is not chilled. It is served at *cellar* temperature, ideally 54 or 55 degrees F (not, as the common misconception has it, at *room* temperature, which would be considerably warmer). For many a doubting American or European traveler, one visit to an English pub is enough to eliminate concerns about "warm beer."

Because any beer—lager or ale—requires yeast for the production of alcohol and carbon dioxide from the malt sugars, the beverage is a living organism at some point in its manufacture. Early breweries engineered the first stage of fermentation in large open vats; the beer was then transferred

into barrels, or casks, and corked tightly. Continuing action of the yeast produced a carbonated or "conditioned" beverage, because the gas in the sealed cask was forced into solution rather than released into the atmosphere.

"Modern" beers, especially in America, are pasteurized and contain no live yeast when they leave the brewery. They are thoroughly filtered (for clarity and "brightness") and carbonated artificially before bottling.

Real English ale, however, is still "cask-conditioned." This makes for a naturally carbonated, delicately flavored, and rather perishable drink. Typically, your pint glass will show a

*Roasted barley malt ready for use at the brewery.*

tiny spot of sediment at the bottom and a faint cloudiness—signs that you're drinking the real thing.

Traditional beer in England has only four ingredients: barley malt, water, hops, and yeast—used in that order. Malt begins as barley "corns." The grain is steeped in water and spread out upon a "malting floor" to a depth of three or four inches. In about a week, when the barley has germinated but before the actual sprouts appear, the process is stopped by gentle heating. When completely dry, the malted barley is roasted. Time and temperature determine the flavor and color of the beer. Most breweries take delivery of the roasted malt in large burlap sacks, packed by malt-sters. Some brewers, such as Guinness, roast their own malt.

At the brewery, the malt goes through roller mills and is made into grist. Water (brewers always call it "liquor") is added, and the grist and liquor are mixed together in a *mash tun*, like a giant pot of tea, at a carefully controlled temperature of 150 to 152 degrees F. The heat is just enough to make the malt en-zymes complete the conversion of starch into water-soluble sugars. The sweet mixture is called *wort*. After two hours the wort is drained through a sieve and rinsed or *sparged*, to extract the maximum amount of sugars. Used grains are sold as cattle feed.

Hops are next. They are added to the wort and the mixture is boiled for one to two hours, traditionally in large, gracefully domed *coppers*. The hopped wort is cooled and filtered

through a radiator, or heat ex-changer, called a *paraflow*. Used hops are sold as fertilizer.

The last and vital ingredient is yeast. Originally, it was literally thrown into the hopped wort, cooled now to about body tem-perature; today this step of brewing, though more scien-tific, is still called *pitching*. Brew-ers cultivate and protect their particular strains of yeast with great care, preserving them

batch after batch. Bass Ale is brewed with a strain that is more than 150 years old.

The fermented wort is skimmed to remove a frothy layer of active yeast. Some of the yeast drawn off is saved for future brews and most is sold as yeast extract (Marmite, for example). In about six days, fermentation is finished. If all the sugar is converted to alcohol, the beer will be strong but thin; if too

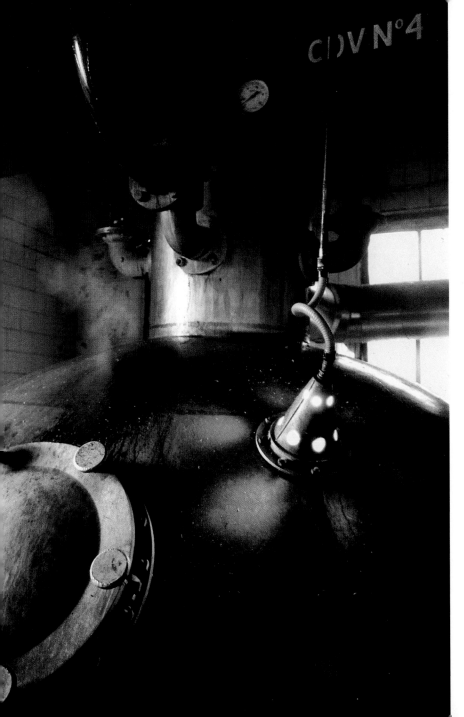

*Hops give ale its characteristic "bitter" flavor and act as a preservative.*

little is converted, it will be weak and sugary. The degree to which the malt sugars are allowed to convert to alcohol is called *attenuation* and averages 75 percent of available sugars.

Before hopped wort is pitched (before yeast is added and fermentation begins), its gravity is measured. The gravity of pure water is designated as 1000; with dissolved and fermentable sugars, a yeast-ready wort will have an *original gravity* of 1030 to 1050. This figure represents the potential maximum strength, and "OG" figures are becoming common as an index of a beer's potency. When the brewmaster stops fermentation, a measurement of *final gravity* (FG) is made. Alcohol content can be determined by subtracting FG from OG and dividing by 8. For example, an OG of 1048 attenuated at an FG of 1012 equals 36; divide

*After pitching, the yeast is skimmed from the top of the wort.*

by 8 and the alcohol content is 4.5 percent by weight. Traditional ales run from 3.5 to 4.5 percent.

After fermentation and gravity measurements, the beer is drawn into conditioning tanks, with the remaining yeast still alive and metabolizing the remaining sugar. The brewer adds a clarifying agent called finings, made from the swim bladders of sturgeon—a process introduced in the seventeenth-century. Finings work by mechanical rather than chemical means—they settle to the bottom of the tank and carry bits of sediment with them. The beer is then "racked" into casks and delivered to the pub. Storage is to be at 55 degrees, and casks must stand for two days to allow sediment to settle properly. Once opened, the beer will remain in peak condition for three to five days.

# The Campaign for Real Ale (CAMRA)

Over the centuries, the English pub has always been defined by the needs of the community surrounding it. No clearer example could exist than the emergence of CAMRA, the Campaign for Real Ale, a story that involves history, politics, and chemistry. In 1976 the National Consumer Council declared CAMRA "the most successful consumer organization in Europe." The group was founded in 1971 by four disgruntled but imaginative journalists. In four years, membership had zoomed to thirty thousand. CAMRA's accomplishments, simply put, have been the preservation of traditional, cask-conditioned "real" ale in England and the reversal of marketing efforts by the giant brewery conglomerates to phase out real ale in favor of keg beer.

Between 1960 and 1970, the number of brewing companies shrank from 250 to fewer than 100, and the number of breweries was halved from 350 to 177. Most important, the mergers of this decade established the now-famous "Big Six"—Bass Charrington, Allied, Watney Mann, Courage, Whitbread, and Scottish and Newcastle. The number of Big Six pubs rose from sixteen to forty thousand in this period—from 24 to 56 percent of all the pubs in England. In 1972 the Big Six produced more than 70 percent of all beer consumed. Today the figure is close to 90 percent.

Mergers or takeovers have occurred for various reasons. In some cases a small brewery was poorly managed and would succumb for essentially "normal" reasons of economic Darwinism. In other cases an already huge firm's desire to become even bigger was expressed in an active search for new acquisitions rather than a passive absorption of nonprofitable ones.

British financial and management experts generally point to an attempted 1959 takeover at Watney's as a significant turning point. Although Watney's management rejected the offer of £21 million, the prospect of actually being taken over frightened them, and their course of action was to get bigger, as quickly as possible, to prevent a merger from ever happening. Naturally, the other horses in the same corral panicked as well.

Another reason for the growing domination of the larger firms (more widely quoted, for obvious reasons) is the now-familiar phrase "economy of scale."

Through advertising, a large national brewery could build a large national market and proceed to sell a national product. This is where chemistry gets involved.

Traditional beers are perishable. To become carbonated naturally, they must ferment in their casks; they must be handled and stored carefully and only for a limited period; they must  be consumed quickly after opening; and, owing to the presence of live yeast, the equipment that dispenses them must be cleaned meticulously and regularly. When England was dotted with small breweries, each serving pubs within a small radius, traditional beer

was appropriate. But with the increasing centralization of the 1960s, traditional beer became an obstacle to "progress."

Chemistry created an alternative in keg beer—a barrel processed at the brewery, its contents pasteurized (to kill the

yeast), filtered (sometimes through sheets of asbestos), artificially carbonated, and dispensed by external gas pressure rather than by hand pump. Simply for reasons of convenience, publicans were often persuaded to offer keg beers instead of traditional ales.

The new keg beers were essentially nonperishable. As a result, they could be transported from huge, centralized production facilities with no complications. Keg beer was, and is, cheaper to produce and higher priced. Between 1966 and 1976, the number of different beers available in England was halved —from three thousand to fifteen hundred. Keg beer sales rose from 1 percent of the market in 1959 to nearly 20 percent in 1976.

The Big Six each introduced a national brand of keg beer and began marketing it aggressively —Watney's Red Barrel, Whitbread's Trophy, Allied's Double Diamond, and so forth. Many pubgoers found these keg beers flavorless and "gassy." Cask-conditioned beers average a carbonation ratio of 1:1 (one pint

of dissolved $CO_2$ per pint of ale); in keg beers the ratio is upwards of 1:5.

When CAMRA was formed, beer drinkers were already showing signs of unrest and were ready for a rallying point. In the second year of the campaign's existence, a monthly newsletter, *What's Brewing*, began to appear, and it hammered away at the undesirable (in the eyes and palates of England's beer drink-

ers) changes and diminishing choice. Many of CAMRA's stories were picked up by the national press. Brian Glover, current editor of *What's Brewing*, says that much of the credit for CAMRA's initial explosion of publicity goes to Richard Boston, whose weekly *Guardian* columns publicized CAMRA and the issues of the day.

Boston had this to say about the Big Six: "Instead of responding to the demands of the market, these large corporations on the contrary accommodate the consumer to their needs. Instead of producing what the people are asking for, they come up with something that is convenient to produce and then, with the help of massive advertising and sophisticated sales techniques, create a demand for it. What enables

them to do this is the sheer quantity of their production, which establishes the norm and thereby sets the fashion."

The annual *Good Beer Guide* made its first appearance in 1971 and was an instant success. Original gravities of all beers in the U.K. were listed. The Big Six had always refused to release this information. This information exposed an essential contradiction of keg beer—higher price but lower strength.

In 1975, just four years after its inception, CAMRA began turning the tide. The Courage Brewery reintroduced its all-but-extinct Director's Bitter (a traditional ale) to sixty pubs in London and Reading. Watney's (mercilessly labeled "Grotney's" in CAMRA's cartoons), which had entirely eliminated cask-

conditioned beer from its pubs in large areas of the country in favor of Red, its keg alternative, reversed its centralization process, resurrecting local names and putting a cask-conditioned beer (tested and approved by CAMRA) in its London pubs. In 1979, Watney's withdrew Red from the market completely.

CAMRA not only reversed the

marketing and brewing trends of the Big Six; it also revived the fortunes of the small regional breweries that had managed to survive the takeover and merger frenzy of the 1960s. CAMRA sparked something of a renaissance in home-brew pubs, whose ranks had slipped to only four in 1974. "When we were settin' up our brewin', they came 'round every week with

advice," says Rita Nicholson of the Fox and Hounds. "They couldn't do enough for me."

CAMRA also functioned legislatively, as a lobbying force, presenting papers to various government bodies. The 1977 Price Commission report on beer prices and profit margins reflected many of CAMRA's arguments against the so-called economy of scale. The Price Commission found that the Big Six's average margin on national sales was 10.6 percent; sixty-nine small, regional brewers showed a margin of 16.3 percent—and were charging lower prices.

CAMRA's founders have all moved on, and membership has leveled off at about twenty-three thousand. The revolutionary bloom has faded because the cause has been largely successful; now, at CAMRA headquarters in St. Albans, six full-timers handle the largely bureaucratic functions of what Brian Glover calls "a very successful non-profit company."

Asked if CAMRA's on-going objective was to preserve the small brewery making real ale or merely the ale itself, Glover replied immediately: "Both. Following a takeover, if the beer stayed exactly the same, and the brewery stayed exactly the same, you could argue that there'd been no change. But it's our experience that that doesn't happen."

Most of the organization's labors currently involve either its monthly newsletter, *What's Brewing*, or its annual publication, *The Good Beer Guide*. The latter is enormously successful and generates a large part of CAMRA's income. Compiled from information forms placed in the hands of pubgoing CAMRA members (nonprofessionals), *The Good Beer Guide* is map-indexed and lists opening hours, beers, and such facilities as food, music, outdoor tables, camping, parking, and games for five thousand pubs. There are still a hundred and fifty CAMRA branches scattered around England as well as CAMRA "brewery liason officers" assigned to every major brewery.

For the time being, the position of cask-conditioned "real ale" is secure. It amounts to about one pint in six of national sales. Whether the next two decades of English brewing will be as newsworthy as the past two remains to be seen. But a possible villain is on the horizon: lager beer. In the 1960s, lager sales amounted to a tiny fraction of national consumption; in 1971 the figure was 10 percent, and by 1980 nearly 30 percent. Predictions call for lager's eventually taking half of national sales.

British lager is a good imitation of ice-cold, relatively flavorless American beer but is a poor imitation of Continental lagers. Like keg beers, lager has superior transport and storage potential, and it brings higher profits. The large brewers are marketing it aggressively, just as they did keg beers. It is possible that, given sufficient sales of lager, the large brewers will again try phasing out traditional beers. Unfortunately for CAMRA, if this shows signs of happening the job of preventing it will be more difficult. Lager differs from keg in one important area—there really is a demand for it. Still, as *Management Today* writer David Manasian concludes, "The big brewers appear to have learned their lesson. CAMRA's very existence still serves as a constant warning to overzealous marketing men in any industry who try to push traditional consumer tastes aside too far, too fast."

# A Small Regional Brewery

Bass Charrington, the biggest of England's Big Six brewers, has nearly ten thousand tied houses scattered throughout England. The Blue Anchor Brewery, a home-brew pub in Helston, Cornwall, has one house—its own. In between are more than a hundred "small" operations. Brakspear's, in Henley-on-Thames, is a sixth-generation family business with 129 tied houses, all within a ten-mile radius of the brewery. Their beers are regarded as excellent, and many of their pubs epitomize the lovely, rustic stuff of which postcards are made. The brewery is a handsome addition to the already picturesque town of Henley. Inside is everything from classic copper mash tuns to modern computers. In 1979,

celebrating the company's two-hundredth anniversary, the directors retained editor Francis Sheppard (former mayor of Henley) to write a history of the brewery.

Robert Brakspear began in 1779 by joining a firm of "common brewers" (innkeepers whose skill had led them to full-time beer making); in 1781 he became a partner. Although 1779 is the official listed date of the founding of the brewery, it was not until 1803 that Brakspear bought out his partners and rightfully gave the firm its present name.

Brakspear retired in 1812 at the age of sixty-two. The brewery then averaged about six thousand barrels a year. These were the "pre-Pasteur" times, when the functioning of yeast was not

fully understood. Mr. Sheppard, quoting from Robert Brakspear's personal brewing journals (still kept at the brewery, in an old hat box), notes this philosophical entry: "Such is the difficulty of conducting this Art [fermentation] to its highest state of perfection, that

even admitting we have obtained the Utmost Rule of Rectitude, we shall yet be liable to error unless thoroughly acquainted with the Nature and Quality of that essential Agent, yeast; and even the most accurate and nicely established Rules must often fail in pro-

*Robert Brakspear's eighteenth-century brewing journals.*

ducing the promised effect." Robert was succeeded by William Brakspear, who was able to steer the operation past financial uncertainty and political skirmishes with other brewers in the area (using what Sheppard calls "typical Victorian business methods") to an "impregnable" position. William entered the business on borrowed capital and owned only nine pubs, with leases on a few others; at the time of his death Brakspear's owned eighty houses, had refurbished their brewery, and was on solid financial ground.

At the beginning of the nineteenth century, Brakspear's was run by William's two sons, Archibald and George, who composed "the third generation of the Brakspear brewing dynasty." The brothers endured rocky times with an uneven performance record, but they did achieve a vital takeover in 1896, buying out the nearby Grey's Brewery. This brought the company's list of pubs to one hundred and fifty, more than they currently own.

In the 1960s, when brewery expansion was at its peak and takeovers were common, Brakspear's was severely threatened. Some of the offers made to shareholders were hard to refuse, and, according to Sheppard, a single anonymous speculator "threatened to make a takeover bid, gain control of the firm, and then close the brewery and sell the pubs at a handsome profit." The company approached Whitbread and arranged sale of a "substantial

A Brakspear's workman checks the mash tun.

minority share" (27 percent) and two directorship seats. With this the firm avoided the very real possibility of dissolution.

Sheppard reports that Whitbread exerts "no policy control" at Brakspear's today. The present brewmaster, Michael Parsons, says the same thing. The brewery is planning an expansion and has enlisted Whitbread's design assistance, but, as Parsons observes dryly, "If we were planning to sell, or were worried about being taken over, we wouldn't be adding to our facility, would we?"

The difference between the products of large and small breweries arises, as Sheppard suggests, from "what the small firms do *not* do to their beer"—a reference to additives such as potato starch, rice, formaldehyde, polymethyl siloxane, and h-heptyl p-hydroxyl benzoate. Brakspear's continues to use only malt and hops, both premium grade and in original (not syrup or pellet) form, with their own yeast, in producing four traditional beers: Old and Mild Ale, and Special and Ordinary Bitter. They also make, but do not advertise, a keg beer (pasteurized and filtered) called Beehive. Brakspear's current annual output is about thirty-thousand barrels, and the company is healthy. In 1975, when national production fell by 3 percent, Brakspear's rose by 14 percent. The firm is gradually offering food in more of its pubs, in response to increasing demand, and has quietly formed a subsidiary called Tabard Inns to provide for some of its larger and more popular houses.

Every year at Christmas Brakspear's procures a sprig of holly and a bunch of mistletoe from the Henley area. On Christmas morning, the yard foreman climbs a special ladder to the top of a special roof eave, and —on a special hook—replaces the old year's cuttings with the new. The mistletoe and holly are visible from the east side of the brewery office building in New Street, Henley. According to Brakspear tradition, if the Christmas cuttings hang securely throughout the year, then the firm will prosper. To date they have never fallen.

# A Guinness, Please

Guinness enjoys a reputation that is, in a sense, the goal of every manufacturer. The company brand name is so familiar and so fully accepted that it has become, in effect, a generic name. Rarely in a pub will one hear a customer ask for "a pint of stout." Invariably, it's "a Guinness, please."

Ask the brewmaster at any brewery his or her opinion of this dark, richly flavored, creamy-headed beverage, and you will more than likely get a response like this (after a measurable pause): "Well, it's . . . certainly unique. There's nothing else like it." Or, "Well, it's the real thing, sort of, isn't it?" Or, "Well, you've got a

bloody good drink there, haven't you?" Even the label, unchanged for more than a hundred years, is considered a classic—more than one up-market advertising firm in California keeps a bottle of Guinness on its shelves as a model for the design of new beer labels.

Guinness is a descendant of a dark ale made with roasted malt that first appeared in London in the 1770s and was popular with Covent Garden workers, whose trade gave the drink its first (and technically still proper) generic name: porter. Dubliner Arthur Guinness had his own brewery for nearly twenty years when, upon returning from London in 1775, he decided to try a batch of the new London dark ale. On his decision, as a Guinness

brochure unabashedly states, "rests the largest porter and stout brewery of all time."

Things have changed (another popular company expression) since Arthur's death in 1803. The original brewery in Dublin now has six counterparts: one in London, and others in Nigeria, Cameroon, Ghana, Malaysia, and Jamaica. The wooden barrels so loved by

James Joyce have been replaced by gleaming tank trucks and specially built rail and overseas transport containers. Arthur's original Dublin brewery occupied a single acre and featured "stables for twelve horses and a loft for 200 tons of hay"; today the St. James's Gate operation is the largest in the world (sixty-five acres, with parking lots probably taking up more space than the original facility). The

first-ever shipment of Guinness was six and a half barrels. Current production is given in such terms as "7 million glasses daily, worldwide" or (from the Park Royal Brewery in London) "a million pints a day."

Things *have* changed. But one thing has not, at least not detectably, and that is the flavor of the beverage. Maintaining the quality of Guinness, and maintaining it consistently, is what underlies all the production data and statistics.

The giant brewery in Park Royal, built in 1937, employs eleven hundred people. They appear well cared for and happy with their place of work—everyone gets a free lunch. Guinness workers maintain quality and flavor by a combination of controls on three

*Guinness's test lab is a hundred meters from the roasting oven. Every brew is evaluated by both human palate and chemical analysis.*

*The Park Royal Brewery is built on a slope. Guinness is flowed, not pumped, through the pipes to the packing department.*

vital factors: raw materials, brewing, and packaging.

Guinness uses primarily hops grown on their own land (a fraction are imported from Yakima, Washington). To protect the delicate resins, the firm stores the hops in a temperature- and humidity-controlled windowless room, which is finished with redwood paneling and herringbone parquet floors. A minimum of six months' supply is on hand at all times. The malt, also a minimum of six months' supply (roughly eighteen tons), is stored in six-story silos inside the brewery. This part of the plant is vacuumed hourly to prevent contamination.

Guinness has no special secrets about either raw materials or procedure. "It's not like Coca-Cola, where they have secret ingredients," says a Guinness public relations man with a smile. "But an awful lot of experimentation and expertise goes into this stuff."

The key step in making Guinness is the roasting of the malt, which gives the color and (along with hops) flavor. The Park Royal brewery has a large rotating roasting oven (the same type used by Nestlé's for coffee) with propane burners underneath. Times and temperatures are monitored automatically and displayed on a control panel with buttons and winking lights. But the roasting is deemed right only when chief roaster Dick Power, with twenty-eight years of experience, has pulled a handful of hot malt kernels from the oven, cut them open, and checked their color and hardness. "Ye can't roast it too quick," he says. "And ye can't roast it too slow." The tool used for this

*The proper tool for the job: roasted barley corns are cut in half to check for color and doneness.*

operation, which looks like a nineteenth-century garlic press, is stored in the left pocket of Power's wool overcoat.

Brewing is continuous at the Park Royal Brewery, with workers on three shifts. The actual beverage that leaves the brewery is the result of blending at least three separate brews. These are tested by both human palate and a process called High Pressure Liquid Chromatography (HPLC). Because of careful monitoring during roasting and before blending, and because Guinness leaves the brewery in large tanks (only in-house bottling—a tiny supply for company use—is done on the premises), the flavor of an individual pint never varies to any measurable degree. But popular belief has it that Dublin Guinness is the best. "Aye, that's true, it is," says Paddy O'Reilly, the Park Royal tour guide. However, Mr. O'Reilly will not comment on exactly why this is true.

In England, draft Guinness is pasteurized (rendering the yeast inactive) and served under very low pressure. Nitrogen as well as carbon dioxide is used—giving the soft, creamy head. Irish draft Guinness is unpasteurized and arrives at the pub in containers known as "iron lungs." Bottled Guinness is a traditionally packaged ale, with live yeast and a tiny spot of sediment at the bottom.

Guinness Brewing is a highly successful corporation (1982 pretax profits were $42 million), with numerous subsidiaries and diversified interests (candies, inns, real estate, photo products, plastics, and infant items). In economic strength the firm is easily on a par with the Big Six brewers. But Guinness, unlike the Big Six, has no pubs. In the late eighteenth and early nineteenth centuries, when other large companies were strengthening their positions by buying houses, Guinness managers strengthened theirs by concentrating on increasing distribution. Today draft Guinness is available in more than 55 percent of England's seventy thousand pubs.

# Architectural Styles

From the elaborate Victorian detailing of the Black Friar, in central London, to the beguiling simplicity of such thatched-roof cottages as the Smith's Arms, in Devon, pubs show a diverse range of architectural styles. The use of regional building materials perpetuates local character and gives area pubs a stylistic link transcending time. Around the Thames Valley, for example, the traveler can enjoy a pint in pubs dating from 1630 to 1930; many of these public houses feature a rugged combination of red brick and milky gray flint. In the Cotswolds, one finds pubs and even entire villages built with huge blocks of sandstone. Colors range from a pale gray (in Bath and environs) to a creamy gold. Half-timber construction utilizing massive oak beams and mortar or brick can

*The George, Winchcombe*

be seen almost everywhere, recalling the days when much of England was covered with prime hardwood forest.

The pub began as an extension —in some cases a conversion— of the private home. While all homes are similar on the most basic architectural level, each manages to be unique. So it is with pubs. There are no franchised look-alikes.

*The Angel on the Bridge, Henley-on-Thames*

*The Dog and Badger, Medmenham*

"The word 'pub' is the most compressed piece of shorthand in the world. The village pub is a drinking house, a parish parliament, and a club rolled into one."
TIMOTHY FINN, *The CAMRA Good Beer Guide*

*The Jolly Miller, Worplesdon*

*The Black Friar, London*

The Perch and Pike, South Stoke

The John Barleycorn,
Goring

The Royal Oak,
Barrington

39

*The Duke of Wellington, Burton-on-the-Water*

*The Thornton Arms, Everton*

*The Flower Pot, Aston*

"When you have lost your inns, drown your empty selves, for you will have lost the last of England."
HILAIRE BELLOC

High Street, Nettlebed

*The Albert,*
*London*

*The Wheatsheaf,*
*Abingdon*

# PUBLICANS & PUB LIFE

What makes a perfect pub? Any brewer will tell you it's the one with the perfect tenant. Customers will say they chose their favorite pub because they liked the publican or the atmosphere. Ultimately, the publican is responsible for the success or failure of a pub, and breweries consider their appointments carefully.

From the customer's side of the bar, it might seem that the publican's job amounts to little more than cheerfully exchanging jokes and treating friends to drinks, but the operation of a pub is a precise business requiring diverse talents and special skills. More than one couple, underestimating the job, have lost their health, their investment,

and in some cases their marriage. Even with a spouse to share the responsibility (this is a common arrangement, and one preferred by the breweries), the profession of publican is best described by the noun *work*. One of many specific problems is trying to find time off. The licensing of pubs in England involves a set of opening and closing-hour regulations that at times confuse both the publican and the staunch regular.

Originating with the Defence of the Realm Act in 1915—initiated primarily to control drunkenness in the munitions factories—these rules set down the hours during which pubs could sell intoxicating beverages: nine hours a day in the realm (but nine and half in London) beginning no earlier than 10:00 A.M. and ending no later than 11:00 P.M., with an afternoon break of no less than two hours. Already a confusing arrangement for a country of regular drinkers, these laws have become diabolically complex, since local justices can alter permitted hours in their districts (for example, by shifting one hour of open time from morning to evening). The result is unpredictable changes from one village to the next. Hours also vary on Sundays, holidays, and village market days, so even among the serious regulars, drinking hours are a continual muddle. Pubs are allowed to *open* at any time, but can sell alcoholic beverages only during the prescribed hours and generally open and close accordingly.

However the hours are determined, the customer has a ten-minute period following closing to finish any previously ordered drink. This grace period, known as "drinking-up time," is marked by the bartender calling "Time, gentlemen, please," or, more currently, simply "Time." When meals are being served, one has a thirty-minute period to finish an accompanying drink.

Opening hours continue to be a national issue of regular debate inside the pub and out. Numerous bills suggesting the liberalization of licensing laws have come before Parliament, but all have met opposition from both publican and consumer groups. It appears that these confusing rulings will remain with us for some time.

# Life at Ye Olde Bell

Val and Keith Wells-West run Ye Olde Bell, a Brakspear's tied house in Henley-on-Thames. The original part of the pub, about four hundred years old, is a timbered, low-ceilinged bar that is quite small—somewhere between cramped and cozy, depending on the time of day. Two dining rooms in the rear are relatively recent additions. The old part of the pub was built with recycled ship's timbers, a common building material in sixteenth-century Henley.

Val and Keith provide food (traditional English, and lots of it) four nights a week, and luncheon daily. Operating Ye Olde Bell requires a seven-day week, and if it weren't for afternoon closing, it would take twenty hours in each of those days. After nearly seven years Val and Keith have worked out a careful routine. Cooking begins at 8:30 in the morning, in a 10- by 15-foot kitchen (smaller than some used to prepare food for a family of four). Typically, this involves cooking twenty to thirty pounds of potatoes (peeled mechanically) and baking a dozen loaves of bread (kneaded with a food processor). For several hours, factorylike noises and appetizing smells permeate the rear of the pub. Val and Keith share the food-preparation chores equally.

On weekends, they serve seventy meals at midday and about fifty for supper. The menu changes every day, and everything is made on the premises—"except the cheesecake," says Val, "because I couldn't make it any better." The food is hearty and reasonably priced.

47

The pub opens at 10:00 A.M. Jim, the barman, greets early arrivals and serves sandwiches. At noon Val stops working in the kitchen and goes upstairs to "get dressed." She reappears in fifteen minutes and the food serving begins. Keith takes drink orders, moving from table to table with incidental items and replenishing supplies from the kitchen. Val, stationed behind a loaded buffet, dishes up meals, takes money, gives change, and, in a marvel of orchestrated labors, makes minor conversation with Olde Bell customers—mainly regulars known by name.

"We had a funny time the other day, didn't we?" says Val. "We often cook a chicken dish, *coq au vin*. One day we tried something a bit new—chicken *espagnol*. We have some young girls working here, you know, they're still at school and all . . . and one of them tasted the chicken and said, "Oh, I think this cocker spaniel's lovely!'"

Luncheon meals are served until 2:30 and the pub closes at 3:00. After collecting the dirty dishes and dismantling the heating table, Val and Keith leave further cleanup to part-time help and go upstairs for a nap.

At 6:00, they come back downstairs to prepare for supper. The pub opens at 7:00. Evening meals are a sit-down affair with candlelight. Val and Keith work together waiting and serving from the kitchen, bustling back and forth past one another with trays and platters, in a sometimes packed dining area.

Food service stops at 10:00 P.M., sometimes earlier depending on traffic. Official closing is 11:00. Neither Val nor Keith works on Sunday night. At noon they serve a traditional Sunday lunch, with a large roast beef.

When do they go to bed? "When we get there."

Do they have time off? "Not really. We try to stay upstairs one or two nights a week, but often as not someone comes in and says, 'We want to see you . . . we've come all this way to see you'—and you feel you've got to come down."

Val and Keith try to find two weeks a year for vacation, though never in the summer, their busiest time. In 1983, they went to Morocco for two weeks in October. "When we do stop," says Val, "we stop in style."

When Val and Keith took Ye Olde Bell, in 1977, their duties included providing Bed and Breakfast, but they soon stopped. "We did it because the previous couple had done it," says Keith. "I think they had long-distance lorry drivers up there or something. It was a bit scruffy. Just wasn't us." Upstairs, the pub has five tiny rooms, typical of sixteenth-century architecture. One is leased to Jim, the barman, and the rest constitute home for Val and Keith. There is one bathroom. This key facility was an important reason that the "Bed and Breakfast" sign no longer hangs at the Bell.

"The biggest drawback," says Val, "was that the money from the rooms wasn't sufficient that we could hire someone and say, 'You come in and change the sheets . . . you come in and cook breakfast.' I had to do it all myself.

"And with that one bathroom . . . all it took was someone to want a bath when I needed to get up, and I couldn't. It just didn't work."

How long will Val and Keith be at Ye Olde Bell—ten years, twenty? "Not twenty," says Keith. Val laughs. "But we'll be here until we retire, certainly."

# Two Home-Brew Pubs

*The Bridgewater Arms*

In 1880, there were twelve thousand home-brew pubs in England. In 1914 the figure was fourteen hundred. In 1966 there were seven, and in 1974 (when CAMRA was just gaining momentum) there were only four. There will never again be a great many pubs that offer beer brewed on the premises, but the home-brew pub, a direct descendant of the original ale-house, has survived.

Currently, there are more than forty. A few are novelty or promotional efforts by big brewers, and a few use the short-cut of malt extract, but the majority of home-brew pubs are the creations of energetic (and often eccentric) individuals who are able to make their operations pay for themselves and enjoy the autonomy and satisfaction that result.

The Fox and Hounds, in Barley (near Royston, Hertfordshire), is a free house owned by Mrs. Rita Nicholson. Mrs. Nicholson, a brassy and extremely sociable Londoner who exemplifies the truism about the nicest pubs being run by the nicest publicans, was a social worker by profession. She became a publican to support her family and disabled husband and has had the Fox and Hounds since 1978.

Mrs. Nicholson was "doing all right" with the pub before trying home brew, but she says she "needed something more." On a visit to a Norwich pub, she indulged in a pint of bitter (a rare experience for her) and found it not only delicious but very cheap. When she asked how such a thing was possible, she was informed that the beer was made on the premises. And this was her inspiration.

"That was it," she says. "I said right there, 'I want a brewery! That's what I want to do!'

We came back and started askin' questions and found the only brewery we could get was about £50,000. And I said, 'Well, damn that.'" Mrs. Nicholson's friend from Norwich came by and said he could "knock one up for a few thousand," which he proceeded to do. It was primitive, and, when

finished, it was unfinished. "We *limped* our way through the first year," she says. "We was springin' leaks everywhere, and the cooler wasn't any good, and we was jackin' hunks of ice in it. It was really hard work. Brewin' day, we was exhausted by nine o'clock." This was in 1980. Today Mrs. Nicholson and her

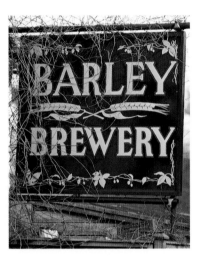

"brewer," Peter, have things under firm control.

Their brewing vessels are secondhand (from Whitbread); a new stainless steel cooler and a refrigerated cellar have been added for summer. Mrs. Nicholson was unable to settle on a name for the operation until a Fox and Hounds regular suggested she give "a bit o' fame" to the local community. So she opted, appropriately, for the Barley Brewery. Peak production is five eighteen-gallon barrels a week.

The Fox and Hounds offers three home brews: Old Pharaoh (named for the original pub in Barley, which burned); Hogshead (a medium-gravity bitter); and Nathaniel's Special (a full-flavored but mild ale). The latter name comes from the vernacular for weak beer (or tea)—"gnat's pee."

Mrs. Nicholson is almost certainly the only woman today who runs a home-brew pub. However, originally—in 1267 anyway, when Henry III issued the Assize of Bread and Ale— women were almost exclusively responsible for the production of beer. They were called "brewsters" or "ale-wives."

Mrs. Nicholson doesn't feel the ranks of on-premises breweries will increase much. "One thing that's spoilin' it a bit is that the big breweries are cashin' in on the idea. Their stuff is beautiful, it's really gorgeous—everything stainless steel and all the rest of it. They wear a suit while they're doin' it. But it's all malt extract, and some of the beer is foul, I mean it's really awful. We use all crushed malt and real hops.

"No, we're not a posh brewery," she says. "Really basic, that's all. But it works. I wanted to do somethin' different. Gives a certain atmosphere to the place, doesn't it?"

Bill Woods, another publican who brews and sells his own beer, shares Rita Nicholson's habit of not drinking it. "I never even knew there were pubs that made their own," he says, recalling his decision to buy the Bridgewater Arms in 1979. "But I remember reading that the place had a brewing license, dating back to 1890, and I thought, 'There must be a gimmick to it.'"

What is now a clean and compact brewery used to be a series of vegetable and cold-storage sheds behind the pub. Mr.

Woods's initial investment in this part of the operation was £25,000. He enlisted a retired brewing engineer from Whitbread to help with design and chemistry and took a four-week course in brewing as well. The Bridgewater Arms uses eighty-gallon stainless steel tanks bought secondhand from Whitbread for the bargain rate of £100 each, with a new boiler.

Is home brewing a difficult art

to learn? "Well," Mr. Woods says, "the man from Whitbread looked at me and said, 'Do you think you could learn to make a steam pudding?' And I said, 'Well, yes . . . I s'pose I could.'" He laughs and adds, "I was stupid enough to believe him!"

Mr. Woods and his son Paul

have a total weekly production of seven to eight barrels. The operation "just about pays." Some of the beer is sold to other outlets. "If I could sell a bit more, it would be great," he says. "But the problem you've got, selling it elsewhere, is the tied house. Not merely tied from the standpoint of the

brewery owning it, but tied financially as well—loans and everything. So you can't get in."

The Bridgewater Arms offers two brews, Best and Special (1035 and 1040 original gravity, respectively). Mr. Woods and son have devised an unusual method of

handling their beer. Only the brew for sale to other outlets is actually racked into barrels; the balance of production is pumped, when ready, directly from the storage tank to the customer's glass, using two pounds of pressure. Mr. Woods explains that this "blanket" pressure is for transport, that it keeps the air out, and that the beer remains free from contamination by wild yeast—a notorious problem for any brewer, large or small. "The secret is keeping everything spotlessly clean," he says. "The beer doesn't come up gassy—it's just got a little more head on it, which is nice."

Mr. Woods feels that offering home-brewed beer at the Bridgewater Arms has helped "a bit" bringing in new customers. Including a restaurant and the brewing operation, the pub employs a dozen people, and enjoys a solid crowd of locals. But Mr. Woods has learned the same lesson from his tiny brewery that the marketing staff at the big breweries learned from management schools: "It takes a heck of a lot of time to get the production right. It's trial and error. It's bloody difficult. You've got to have a brew that's consistent. Acquired taste—that's one of the secrets of this business.

"The economics are difficult, but it's quite good fun. And you know, the head brewers would all love to do this. They've got all those computerized panels and such, and they never really see their brews . . .

"If you can get your customers used to your beer, and if it's good, they won't bloody drink anything else. They won't go anywhere else. That's the whole theory of it."

# Local Character and National Pastimes

 No two of England's pubs are the same. One may be refined, its neighbor rough around the edges; one noisy, the other quiet; one cozy and romantic, the next brightly lit and full of pensioners, carpenters, salesmen, and dogs. Whether empty or full, peaceful or frantic, a pub and its customers combine to produce, at its best, the greatest of English inventions.

A small village might have only one pub, where everyone meets to exchange gossip and catch up on the news. In larger towns one walks to the neighborhood pub for companionship and an evening out. Even in highly urban areas, where there are many pubs that may cater to

a younger crowd, working people, or the professional, a pub's local character remains intact. A good pub is a combination of a cozy living room, a church social, and a marathon toast to the health of all present. After a few visits, one is welcomed as a regular—ordering "the usual" and perhaps sitting down to a game of dominoes in front of the fire.

Besides serving as a social center, the pub has always been associated (often without official approval) with a range of village sports too numerous to record. Henry VII, in 1495, issued the first known national regulation discouraging public houses from allowing indoor games because they were keeping men from archery.

Many traditional pub games have been lost or exist only in

memory, with local variations complicating the already hopeless task of collecting them. Once-popular games such as Merels, Ringing the Bull, Toad in the Hole (also a recipe), Nine Men's Morris, Spoof, Kannoble, Aunt Sally, Flinging the Wellington Boot, and even Dwile Flonking (described by

Richard Boston as "well away from the centre of sanity . . .") seem now to appear sporadically and only in certain areas, with widely differing rules and even purposes.

The more common surviving games—skittles (indoor bowling), dominoes, draughts

(checkers), and darts—are found all over England. Darts is the most popular, played in almost every pub. Little is really known of the origin of darts, but the common theory is that the game began as indoor archery, with the target a wooden cask turned on end. In London, the darts are still often called

"arrers." Certainly the game began in the pub, and in this century has become an international sport, with well over a million registered league players in the British Isles.

Darts in an English pub is an activity demanding two very clearly defined areas of expertise. One, obviously, is the appropriate motor skill required in getting the dart to the target. The other, less apparent, is a remarkable ability to calculate the score by means of faster-than-light subtraction. There may be as many as forty variations of the game currently played in Britain (with up to eleven different target designs), but the basic idea is to begin with a score of 301, 501, or 1001 (the popular standards), reducing the total by the amount thrown each turn, until some-

one ends exactly on zero. Once begun, the game becomes a series of computer-speed calculations (running scores are recorded by the opponent or a third party on a blackboard mounted inches from the target almost before the darts have left the player's hand) and instant decisions on tactics for remaining throws.

Richard Boston, in *Beer and Skittles*, mentions players having reached such a high level of skill that they sometimes make things "more difficult for themselves by playing with sharpened hairpins or six-inch nails, but for you or me (well, me anyway) the ordinary game is quite hard enough . . . If your score stands at 257 and

you throw a treble 17, a 9 and 7, it will impress no one if you add up on your fingers—three seventeens are 51, and 9 is 60, and 7 is 67. It will cut even less ice if you write 67 under the 257, draw a line under it and then subtract. The skilled darts player's arithmetic is as swift as an arrer. Try to get your opponent to do the scoring."

# SIGNS & SIGN WRITERS

The Four Horseshoes is a small village pub in a rural area about forty miles west of London. It marks the junction of two gravel roads. Although the Four Horseshoes is not especially old by English standards (it was built in the mid-eighteenth century and sold a hundred years later to Brakspear's for £600), its hanging wooden sign could date back seven or eight centuries.

The artist who made the sign was aware, perhaps, that his work had refinement and balance, and was painted "correctly"—in England, horseshoes are always shown right side up, so the luck doesn't fall out—but these were not his reasons for omitting the words "Four Horseshoes." When this sign was first painted, most of the people looking at it couldn't

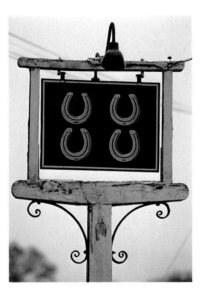

read. Today, with illiteracy the exception and not the rule, the majority of England's more than fifty thousand pub signs include the name of the establishment, the brewery with which it is affiliated, and sometimes additional lines advertis-

ing "Bed and Breakfast" or "morning coffee." The direct pictorial style, however, has survived.

Hand-painted signs, first seen before the end of the tenth century, were once used quite widely—giving literal illustrations (or models) of various trades and products. They were constantly used as travelers' landmarks. With the spread of "learning"—leading to street names, sequential numbering, and postal codes—pictorial signs nearly disappeared. Only pubs and inns retained this form of identification. Why these signs persisted is a mystery, but surely a fortunate one. Ask for directions anywhere in England today, and chances are that a pub ("Look for the sign —you can't miss it!") will be part of the answer.

Pub names, while delightfully varied, have never been determined casually. There is always a story, often associated with something of local historical interest. All walks and forms of life are celebrated, from the King and Queen to the Laboring Man, from Sherlock Holmes to Robin Hood, and nearly an ark's worth of animals—horses, bears, dogs and cats, lions, birds, badgers, snails, tortoises, rabbits, and (of course) unicorns.

The most common sign is the Crown, sometimes in combination with the Rose; second is the Red Lion. Richard Boston notes in *Beer and Skittles* that "pub signs are a good way of keeping children or adults occupied on long car journeys. Various games can be devised. The simplest is for two players to take one side of the road each,

scoring one point for every leg seen on an inn-sign. The Cock thus scores two, the White Horse four. The Fox and Hounds is usually accepted as a knock-out victory."

The artists who paint these signs for a living today have highly individualized approaches to their craft. They compose a small and essentially unknown group entrusted with the preservation of a thousand-year-old national tradition. They lead strangely isolated lives. The brewing of beer has generated literally tons of data —but no one in England knows how many artists earn a living from painting pub signs. There is no annual meeting of sign writers, no newsletter, no union, no national apprenticeship program, and apparently no communication at all among the artists themselves. Rarely have they met or even heard of one another, even by reputation.

The hand-painted pub sign originally had a humble, purely functional role, but centuries of use have established it as a national artistic institution. John Cook, one of England's foremost authorities on signs and sign writing, expresses it succinctly: "These signs are the repository of our social history."

# George Biles

Frederick George Biles was born in 1900 and has been a professional designer and painter of pub signs since the age of twenty-nine. He works five days a week in his airy, two-room studio in Bridport, near Lyme Regis on the south coast. He has no intention of retiring.

"I'm a widower," he says. "My work is all I have, and I enjoy it." Mr. Biles attributes his steady health to diet (only two meals a day and tea in the morning) and abstinence from both alcohol and tobacco.

Mr. Biles has a delicate, subdued style that seems to capture the overcast lighting characteristic of the English seaside. His signs often contain subtle ocean blues and carefully executed grey or cloudy skies. Although he says that horses are his fa-

vorite subject for painting, his strongest work is clearly in a nautical vein—the Cutty Sark in the Ship Inn sign, for example, or the original and touching Three Mariners (normal treatment for this theme is

three sailors doing a hornpipe).

Mr. Biles—he sometimes refers to himself as "professor"—is also a highly skilled calligrapher and produces beautiful illuminated manuscripts. With tremendous pride, he will show a photo-

graph of the Queen at an awards ceremony receiving one of his manuscripts. This work requires excellent eyesight and a steady hand; into his eighth decade, he is still doing it, with a recent assignment scheduled for delivery in Africa.

Though not formally trained, Mr. Biles was always aware of his skills in drawing. He began as an apprentice sign writer at the age of fourteen. Describing his first pub sign, he tells this story: "It was a woman with a shield, a 'Britannia' sort of a

thing. The boss started doin' it, and it looked like a bag o' spuds! I said, 'Well! I can do better'n that!' And there was my first sign." Though Mr. Biles has worked alone most of his career, five apprentices have passed through his studio. One remains in the pub sign business. One had his own business, retired, and died in 1980. "Bigger work" has attracted the others, reports Mr. Biles, including (he says with a trace of a smile) one individual who currently works "painting lines on roads."

When asked about the longevity of his work, Mr. Biles declared without hesitation that "I've had signs last twenty years." One of the signs in his

studio, for the Coach and Horses, was fifteen years old. It was brought in for repairs after being knocked from its hangers.

Having experimented with various signboard materials, including masonite and metal, Mr. Biles has settled on a combination of marine plywood and automotive-type paints as providing the greatest durability. "All a person's got t'do," he says, "is t'keep 'em clean. And twice a year, wax 'em."

Undeniably, economic and cultural trends have had an effect on the future of the hand-painted pub sign. But "the professor" remains as confident of his livelihood as he is of his health. The craft of sign writing, he says, is not an endangered one.

"It's comin' into fashion. It's not

a dyin' art . . . no, it's comin' into fashion, and I'm the one's responsible for bringin' it into fashion in this area. That's a fact. It's not a boast, it's a fact."

# John Cook

"They call me Rembrandt," says John Cook, whose tenure as chief sign painter at the huge Whitbread Breweries spanned more than forty-seven years. "That's sort of a code word. It went from the chairman of the board right on down."

Cook, now retired, began his career at sixteen as an apprentice. He is unquestionably of artistic stock, but his demeanor might be better described as academic. He welcomes you to his office, essentially a continuous wall of file cabinets with a modest desk, and starts pulling out drawers. For every sign leaving the Whitbread studio (there have been thousands) there is a file.

Cook is a tireless and fastidious researcher, and his reputation is so strong that Cambridge Uni-

versity has invited him to lecture on pub signs. He continues this work in retirement, giving evening classes with slides. He is a member of both the English and Canadian societies for heraldry—"the shorthand of history," he calls it.

"The problem," Cook says, "is to simplify. We don't put irrelevant material in our signs. We don't paint those poster things

—where you have to stand right underneath them to know what they are."

"And we don't sign our work. The freelancers have to put their names down, but we don't need to do that."

"We try to make our figures plain and easy to see. This is the difference, you see, between painting a picture for the National Gallery—for posterity —and painting a pub sign. Today, people travel in cars, not on foot or horseback. And signs have to be seen at much greater distances."

Cook's design directives and firm hand made his generation of Whitbread signs (the majority of which are still hanging) an easily recognizable family: simple forms executed with

fairly large brushes, soft colors, and minimal detailing.

His production approach is appropriately systematic. The Whitbread studio in Cheltenham is large (enormous compared with the work spaces of freelance artists) and fully equipped. Cook's apprentices used, and continue to use, an elaborate easel whose counterweights and pulleys allow raising, lowering, and rotating of the work. Cook installed a mirror on the ceiling that gives the artist sitting at the easel a view of the sign as it would appear from a distance of fifty feet.

Whitbread signs are painted on aluminum panels, which, though more prone than wood to peeling, are indestructible and have the advantage of being essentially one-time purchases.

John Cook and Michael Hawkes in the main room of Whitbread's sign studio in Cheltenham.

On the average, they require repainting every nine years.

Michael Hawkes, an apprentice who took command of the studio after Cook's retirement in 1980, seems to represent a blend of Cook's approach and his own, which similarly emphasizes simple, easily recognizable forms, but favors brighter colors and a bit more detailing. In addition, Hawkes has, with Whitbread's blessing,

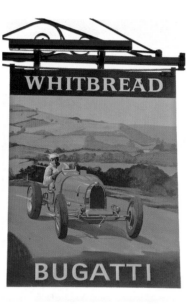

expanded the scope of the studio. Using the name Brewery Artists, Hawkes and his colleagues have produced a promotional brochure listing themselves as creators of original artwork, book covers, lighting, and pictorial signs for everything from "castles to coffeehouses." Whitbread, of course, remains the parent company and is pleased that the studio has expanded and is doing more types of work.

"Our history," says Cook, "goes back to before the Romans—so our subjects can be anything. When you do the research, there is always a reason for a pub's name." For example, from recent history, the Bugatti, in Gretton, commemorates a spe-

cial yearly sports car rally; from far older times, The Flying Monk, in Malmesbury, marks a disastrous attempt by a twelfth-century monk to fly with artificial wings.

"A great many commerical things today, they're painted only for money. And they bloody well look it. Our signs, we like to say, are painted with love and sweat."

# Coleen Burnett

Formally trained as a sculptor, Coleen Burnett came to painting pub signs by means of political coincidence. She lives northeast of Aylesbury in a tiny village that, along with a dozen others, was abruptly faced with destruction because of a proposed airport. She and her neighbors held meetings to organize and protest. They were eventually successful.

In the process (and, she says, more or less by default) Burnett became the group's poster designer. She painted a series of murals, which were installed along the main north–south rail line. Hundreds of passengers traveling between London and Scotland saw her work every day.

"It was huge," she says. "And I mean huge. A farmer in overalls, with his pitchfork across his chest, you know, in a position of utter defiance. And *one* of his eyes took a whole panel of pressed board.

"It stretched along the tracks, with one word, over and over, as the copy: NO. People would zoom alongside, and read the words again and again: NO . . . NO . . . NO . . . NO. That was all."

Ms. Burnett entered art school at the age of thirteen and continued through to college, finishing at twenty-one. She studied the arts generally, but until her experiment with posters, she "leaned more toward clay than paint." However, steady employment as a sculptor is hard to find. And the lesson of conveying a simple,

direct message to a large audience was not lost on her. She began approaching breweries for work as a sign painter.

Initially, she says, it was a case of mutual caution. "They have to get to know you. But when they trust you, and trust your work, it goes fairly easily."

Ms. Burnett's best work involves animals. The irresistible Live and Let Live, for example,

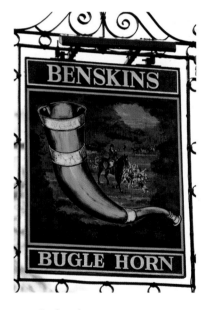

could only have been done by a dog (and cat) fancier. Ms. Burnett is extremely fond of both. At her cottage, she keeps four dogs (all of them lerchers —a leggy, fast breed used for hunting) and an assortment of

cats. In her living room is a handsome fireplace with a carefully executed relief sculpture beneath the mantel—a reclining dog, chin on paws, as if warming himself in front of the fire.

Ms. Burnett estimates her total output simply as "hundreds." The time required for a single sign varies widely. She seems unique in her choice of paint —a polyurethane gloss enamel, turpentine-based, which she says combines the quick drying of acrylics with the brightness and color saturation of oils. Durability, always determined by the English climate, is from five to ten years. Her style is straightforward—"I like the older, traditional things," she says, "but with a bit of modern interpretation." Her Green Man is a combination of traditional elements (garments made of leaves and a torch) and her own imagination.

Her current situation is a familiar artist's dilemma: financial security versus the need for new subjects and experience. She is restless, perhaps bored.

"I don't like the commercial pressure," she says. "The breweries seem to think you can turn them out like shelling peas. That's when it stops being fun.

"If they want their signs to be new and fresh and diverse and exciting, they should go out and hire a range of different artists. That way many different people would be producing many signs, rather than many signs just being pumped out from one individual."

# Stanley Chew

Stanley Chew is a colorful man who makes colorful signs. He and his wife Pauline live on a twenty-acre farm in pastoral Devon. Phoning his home (a fourteenth-century stone farmhouse), you may be advised that he is working in the studio, but just as likely you will find that he is working in the pasture or working in the barn. Mr. and Mrs. Chew savor their rural lifestyle, which includes a large vegetable garden, dairy cows, and frontage with fishing privileges on the River Dart. They take tea in the afternoon with cream that, in the morning, "was still in the cow."

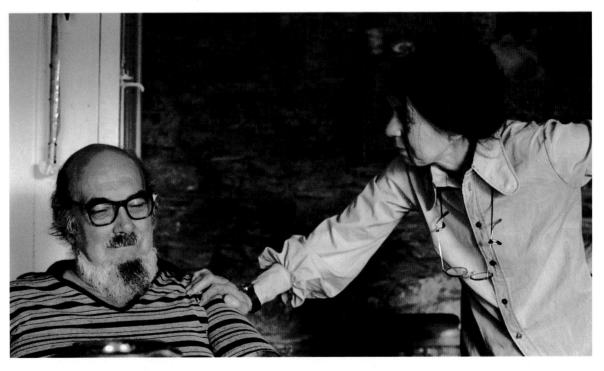

Chew's career as a sign painter began in London in the early 1940s. "I used to paint the signs on lavatory doors," he says with a laugh. "'Ladies and Gents,' 'This Way and That.' There weren't as many pub signs then, and the quality wasn't so high. I saw what was being done and decided that I could do as well.

"I'd go into a pub, and offer to

do their menu. Then their doors, and then their sign. It was very hand-to-mouth.

"After a while, there came a time when the breweries started upgrading their houses. And my business took off a bit." Chew's primary client today is Bass, the largest brewer in England. Chew has "trained" them, he says, to come to him, so that he and his wife rarely need to leave their farm.

His signs are among the country's brightest and most colorful, because he uses oil paints and lots of primary pigments. A newly installed Stanley Chew sign against a weathered sixteenth-century Cotswold stone wall can give an electric, neon effect.

"Yes," he says, smiling. "I do like

the bright colors. It's a bit like stained glass, isn't it?"

Chew's studio is tiny, perhaps fifteen feet square, and did prior service as a farm shed. It has windows affording him a view of the pasture. He is busy, and the studio is a clutter of finished and half-finished signs, tubes

and cans, brushes, and a small library of reference books.

A sign requires about a week for both sides ("I'm horribly slow," Chew says) and will cost the client about £200. Like most other artists, Chew will work on whatever surface the client brings him. His preference is for

KING WILLIAM

Bass

The Dolphin

RED LION

Devenish

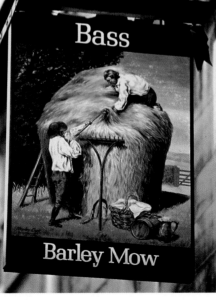

Bass

Barley Mow

Bass

tempered masonite in a wood frame. He finishes each sign with three coats of varnish. Because oil paints are the least weather-resistant, they "need doing" every five or six years.

"There aren't many of us who do this sort of thing," he says. "The breweries don't pay enough, really. It's not a lot of money for one of these signs, but they still think I'm expensive…."

# George Mackenney

Take a close look at one of George Mackenney's signs and it should be clear why he says that his career objective was originally that of portrait painter. The fact that his dream did not come true has been a disappointment to him, but for pubgoers and travelers throughout England, who enjoy the proof of his skills, it's a happier story.

Mackenney's parents were publicans and he was born at their pub in London. He had rickets as an infant and was crippled until the age of four. As a child he had no toys. "But," he says with a proud gleam, "I could always draw. Always." He studied art in London for seven years. Right from the start, he wanted to paint portraits.

At the age of thirty-four,

Mackenney entered a self-portrait in oils in the competition at the Royal Academy in London. He was new, undiscovered, hungry, and one of twelve hundred other artists. He and his new bride Thelma were living in an attic.

"I worked on it for almost two years," he recalls. "I didn't leave one stitch not attended to. My shadows, everything—my technique was superb."

"I was after royalty. That gallery of the Royal Academy is the best showroom window in the world. Once you're accepted there, you never look back. I wanted it desperately." Mackenny had the highest hopes. Had the painting been accepted, a fabulous career would have followed. Top-level portraits of royalty command

prices in the neighborhood of £8000 today.

But after three months, there was still no word from the Academy. Part of the official policy is a silent return of submissions, with no explanation

whatsoever. Mackenney, in describing this experience, is not bitter. But the sense of his disappointment is still keen after more than thirty years.

"If you're not there, if things don't go your way, at that right

moment in history . . . that's it. There's just no going back. I felt, after that rejection at the age of thirty-four, that I just couldn't continue."

But continue he has, and for an audience far wider than royalty. After working briefly in Lon-don for an advertising agency—"a miserable little job"—Mackenney turned to pub signs. He estimates his output to date at "more than five thousand"—making him a good bet for the title of England's most prolific sign writer.

Mackenney uses the same oil-and-turpentine combination preferred for portraits. He works with an old, caked pal-ette and a fistful of brushes. His technique is practiced and efficient. He says it's not un-usual for him to paint in a tie and white shirt. His tiny but well-lit studio usually features an assortment of dogs, cats, and classical music. He consistently produces three signs a week and has done as many as fourteen in a month.

Mackenney will paint on either wood or metal but prefers aluminum; wood, he says, is sure to rot eventually in the English climate. He hires a man to strip and prime the panels, and then gives them two coats of white lead. The fee is from £160 to £230 per sign. His work is guaranteed for five years and normally lasts at least seven, sometimes ten or eleven. About half the work is delivered to his home (a thatch-roof cottage south of Aylesbury) and the balance is picked up. He and Thelma are still married. "She does my books, my taxes, and my records," Mackenney says. "And the research as well. She does everything, really."

SARACENS HEAD

CHARLES WELLS

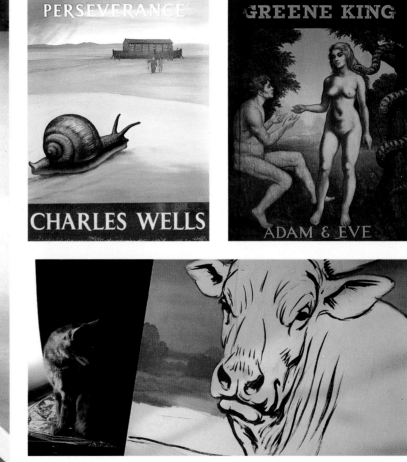

PERSEVERANCE

CHARLES WELLS

GREENE KING

ADAM & EVE

"I'm good. And I enjoy showing off," he says, "because I know I can deliver. British understatement infuriates me. Belittling your achievements—that's typically English, if you ask me. . . . So long as I've got a brush in my hand, I don't care if I'm painting a wall."

# A Sign Sampler

ROYAL OAK
Devenish

ROYAL OAK

HENLEY BREWERY

In a land noted for institutions, the pub is certainly Britain's most durable—having weathered social revolution, political upheaval, and even progress. The signs are a pictorial testimony to this durability.

FREE HOUSE

The Royal Oak

The Royal Oak depicts the seventeenth-century monarch Charles II, who, along with Henry VIII, was the most fabled king in English history. In 1651 Charles II was trying to make his way to safety in Paris after the battle of Worcester. He was helped by several brothers in the Penderel family, who dressed him in simple woodsman's clothing and darkened his face with soot. This part of the story gave rise to a less common sign, The Black Boy—in reality, the disguised king. The Penderel brothers helped Charles II into a huge oak, where he spent a day and a night, sleeping on the spreading branches while his would-be captors searched the woods below. Charles himself dictated this story to Samuel Pepys in 1680, after his return to power. Souvenir hunters literally tore the tree to pieces in the middle of the seventeenth century, and a descendant of the original "royal" oak now marks the spot. As for the Penderel brothers, Charles II did not forget their bravery—he gave them and their family a pension that the family's descendants receive to this very day.

84

The headless woman in this sign is Judith, or Juthware. Her story is told in a fifteenth-century manuscript called the Sherborne Missal. Judith was a seventh-century saint who helped pilgrims on their way to a shrine in the village. Her stepmother and brother, resentful and jealous of the strangers constantly in their home, took her life by sword. According to the legend, she picked up her own head and carried it to the altar before expiring. And her ghost, still carrying its head, haunts the lane on Judith Hill in Halstock.

"Make my image but an

D

# alehouse sign."

SHAKESPEARE, *King Henry IV, Part II*

THE QUEEN

WHITBREAD

VICTORIA

HITBREAD

KE of SUSSEX

WHITBREAD

SHERLOCK HOLMES

89

# PUB FARE

English cooking is changing. Long-forgotten traditional dishes are surfacing on linen-covered tables and inventive new variations of continental recipes are appearing on menus throughout the country. Nowhere is this change more evident than in the pub. Richard Boston's assessment of the Ploughman's Lunch as "the best and worst of pub food" is still true, but the odds of being surprised and delighted with imaginative interpretations of this classic, "simple" pub offering are on a notable increase.

For years, English food has had the reputation of consistently overcooked vegetables, starchy and salty meat pies with no measurable seasoning, greasy

fish and chips, and megacalorie desserts. But forgettable meals are no more common in England than anywhere else. And today many pubs have full-time cooks responsible for varied menus of both original and traditional fare.

According to Norman Rushton of the Chequers, in Fowlmere, the single most important influence in British cooking is (and always has been) the French. After the French Revolution in 1789, many top French chefs found themselves unemployed.

Across the Channel, however, England was creating a solid upper-middle class with money to spend. Communications and transportation were excellent. Many French chefs left their country for a more secure and profitable working environment.

At this time English food was, in Mr. Rushton's terms, "rustic" —inexpensive meat-and-vegetable pies and similar dishes. It became the fashion in wealthy households to have at least one French chef. The flamboyant cooking style and presentation of the French quickly overshadowed the simple, yet often elegant, English cookery of the period. This powerful influence, combined with the effects of the Industrial Revolution and two wars, threatened the native culinary arts with extinction. Mr. Rushton describes these events as "catastrophic."

"This village used to have double its population," he says of Fowlmere.  "Now it's like a dormitory— people sleep here and travel to work. We used to be more like the Chinese. The grandparents were at the head of the family, living with their children and grandchildren. But it's very, very rare today to see three generations of the same family living together —or even close together. And so recipes and cooking techniques aren't handed down any longer. My grandmother used to make her own soup stocks. Now everybody gets it from a can."

World War II pushed England's already weak culinary identity into a depression that seemed irreversible. The austerity essential in wartime developed a heroic practicality in the English heart and a "make do" attitude that was to remain long after the need for painful rationing had ended. People learned, with pride, to get along without fresh foodstuffs and to accept the synthetic substitutes made available. Recipes changed, and so did eating.

Rationing during the war was followed by subsidizing as the country recovered. Free or low-cost meals at work and school contained large amounts of potatoes, milk, and bread, and created a nationwide appetite for plain, starchy foods at cheap prices. Postwar "advances" in farming eliminated many re-

gional specialties by nationally centralizing crop production, and even more traditional cooking was lost. Today, "mass" fast-food chains contribute to the same effect.

By 1950, England's food consciousness was all but extin-

guished and the term "English cooking" fading from the culinary vocabulary. But with a revived economy, the 1950s and 1960s found increasing numbers of English people on holidays abroad. Continental travel— formerly a privilege of the wealthy, who could buy and eat

whatever they desired, in spite of national influences—became routine among the working and middle classes. These travelers often returned home to find their previously comatose taste buds in a state of full alertness. And the first person to hear that eating well was not some

sort of Latin extravagance, but was in fact one of life's most agreeable pleasures, was the local publican.

Predictably, transplanted menus began to spring up in country inns and pubs. The Continental *technique*, however, was slow to develop. All too often, the *Côte de Boef rôti* turned out to be the same old roast beef and the *fromage* a piece of stale cheddar. But the English love of food and drink had been re-awakened. Imitations became more competent. As their confidence increased, cooks, chefs, and researchers began unearthing fragments of old cookbooks, diaries, and journals to discover a cuisine laced with humor and inventiveness.

Today, a wide range of English

cookbooks is available, making a place for "new" as well as traditional cookery. And the quality and selection in many a pub are keeping pace with those of the better restaurants.

"I think the big thing about British food today is that the British chef, himself, is believing in his own ability to cook," says Phillip Harris, of the Three Horseshoes in Madingley. "Over the years, it's been an accepted thing that the British people, as a nation, can't cook. The French can cook, the Italians can cook; the Germans can't cook, the British can't cook, the Irish can't cook. And the Americans can't cook—all you get in America is a bloody great piece of beef that covers your plate, and because they

give you lots, that's enough.

"But now, British food— food, shall we say, prepared by British chefs —is standing up to any international test."

Mr. Harris, whose seventeenth-century thatched-roof pub features an intriguing menu of traditional and new dishes, sees a "new breed" of English chef.

"They've all gone and studied with the masters. But now, they've come back home— young men who have the courage of their convictions, saying, 'Well, if I use my knowledge and apply it to my British food, what can I produce?' You don't need a French name to be able to cook. You can be English and still cook."

93

"The ubiquitous 'Ploughman's Lunch'—bread, butter, cheese, pickled onions—represents the best and worst of pub food."
RICHARD BOSTON, *Beer and Skittles*

The menu at the Chequers, in Fowlmere, is another expression of confidence and imagination that characterize the new British chef. The selection ranges from traditional items, such as Dover Sole, to Grilled Breast of Duckling flamed with cognac and served with a *petite orange* salad. Wines from six countries are available. Produce and meats are delivered daily, some from as far away as New Zealand and Zimbabwe. Even though the Chequers is many miles from any large population center, the pub's atmosphere and excellent menu keep it fully booked ten months of the year.

Besides being an imaginative chef, Chequers's manager Norman Rushton is a thoughtful individual with a good sense of humor and a fascinating perspective on British culinary

## LYMESWOLD CHEESE AND CHIVE FRITTERS

*Norman Rushton,*
*The Chequers*

Served on a bed of hot tomatoes. For four people.

### FRITTERS

1 pound Lymeswold cheese (Camembert or Brie can be substituted)
4 tablespoons white sauce
1 bunch chives
Salt and pepper

The cheese should be at room temperature. With your hands, mix together in a bowl the cheese, white sauce, chives, salt, and pepper. Divide the mixture into 12 equal portions and roll into small balls. Flour, egg, and breadcrumb the balls and deep-fry until golden brown. For the best results, fry the balls quickly in hot oil.

### CHOPPED TOMATOES

4 peeled, diced tomatoes
1 chopped onion
1 tablespoon oil
1 bunch fresh sage

Sweat the onions in oil; do not color. Add the diced tomatoes and a little chopped sage. Bring to a boil and season with salt and pepper.

To serve, cover the bottom of a small plate with the chopped tomatoes. Place the fritters on top and decorate with the remaining fresh sage leaves.

history. "I've got quite bright parents, but I wasn't terribly good at school," he says. "So I took a trade.

"But the ole ticker [he points to his head] still kept going. And I read a lot of course books and such." Mr. Rushton went to cooking school at Westminster Technical College in London and has been a chef all his adult life. He worked in a four-star restaurant in London and has had the Chequers since 1979.

He sees the changes in English cooking as a trend toward lightness: "If you take and look at an Edwardian-era picture —from the days when Britain was strong—all 'gentlemen' were nice and portly and round, with their waistcoats rising up. The poor kids were all scraggly and thin. Anybody in the lower classes, you know, was like a rake. Anybody who was a well-respected figure of a man had a great big pot belly.

"Now today . . . I've got a bloke comes in here—what he hasn't got shares in, I don't know. Property speculator, drives a Roller. He can afford to eat any-where he wants. He's thin as a flippin' rail!"

Mr. Rushton is constantly add-ing new items to his menu, but finds it a difficult business. To persuade people to try his Batons of Chicory and Beetroot Salad, for example, he had to remove the listing for Prawn Cocktail.

"Anything with prawns, most English people today will eat it and ask for nothing else. We had to remove Steak and Chips, too—even though if someone does request it, we'll

be delighted to prepare it— because it would be the only thing we'd sell."

Mr. Rushton has dozens of stories that illustrate the chal-lenging and sometimes frustrat-ing position of a culinary pioneer. A highly respected London chef ordered grouse. The dish was served pink, and the chef angrily sent it back, stating it had not been cooked. A complicated quail prepara-tion (boned, stuffed with pâté, cooked in madeira sauce, sealed in pastry and delivered to the table with a tiny shot of brandy) prompted not a com-pliment, but a sarcastic letter about "sparrows being fobbed off as quail." A top-level

company manager took one bite of his crisp, pencil-thin green beans and sent them back to the kitchen as "raw."

"We're changing and improv-ing," says Mr. Rushton. "But God—it's hard work. Today, most British people will not pay for good food. It's just a tradi-tion, the way they've been brought up. Food is supposed to be free. Seventy percent of our lobsters go to France because British people won't pay for them. It's a funny state of affairs at the moment, really . . . our food is a conglomeration. As the world shrinks, it's inevita-ble. We've got *nouvelle cuisine*, *haute cuisine*, *flambé* work— that's just comin' in—and God knows what else. We're gonna take the best. The trend is still toward lightness. A lot more healthy, isn't it?"

## ROAST PHEASANT
*Norman Rushton, The Chequers*

Served with Bread Sauce and Liver Croutons

1 whole fresh pheasant, cleaned (retain the liver)
  (A white game bird does not require excessive hanging and we
  recommend a pheasant no older than three days.)
2 large rashers of bacon
Oil
Salt and pepper

Season the pheasant with salt and ground pepper. Heat a little oil in a roasting tray and, on top of the stove, seal the bird to a light golden brown. Place the bird on its back and cover the breast with the bacon rashers. Place in a hot oven (approximately 450°F) and cook for approximately 20–25 minutes. Just before the bird is ready, remove the bacon rashers from the bird and brown the breast to a nice golden brown.

### GRAVY
Remove the pheasant from the pan and keep it warm. Pour off the excess fat and add 1 cup of water to the roast juices. Bring to a boil on the stove. Season. Serve in a sauce boat separately.

### BREAD SAUCE
¼ pint milk
2 slices diced white bread
  (without crusts)
Salt

A pinch of grated nutmeg
2 cloves
Butter

Boil all the ingredients together in a pan and whisk to a puree. If it becomes too dry, add more milk. Serve in a sauce boat separately.

### CROUTONS
Quickly fry the pheasant liver in a little oil until they are brown on the outside and pink in the middle. Place the liver on a chopping board and chop fine with a sharp knife. Mix the liver with an equal quantity of softened butter, and season with salt and pepper. Spread this pâté on small slices of toasted French bread and serve around the pheasant.

### SUGGESTED VEGETABLE: matchsticks of leeks
Using only the white of the leeks (the green can be used for stock or soups), cut into thin matchsticks. Fry these quickly in a little butter. Season with salt and pepper. Serve immediately. For the best results, cook them until slightly crisp.

"It's the noise it makes when it hits the pan—can be any green vegetable—a traditional English dish originally to use up leftovers. You squash it all down and it bubbles and squeaks away."
PHILLIP HARRIS, *Three Horseshoes*

## MULLIGATAWNY SOUP
*Phillip Harris, Three Horseshoes*

12 shallots, chopped
2 apples, peeled and chopped
½ pound lentils, soaked overnight
2 ounces butter or oil
1 quart chicken broth
4 cloves garlic, pressed
1 tablespoon curry powder
¼ cup mango chutney
½ cup cooked rice
2 pounds canned tomatoes
2 tablespoons tomato paste
1 small hot red pepper, seeded and chopped, or cayenne to taste
2 cloves
Heavy cream or sour cream

Sauté shallots and apples in butter until lightly brown. Add curry powder, lentils, garlic, and red pepper. Add broth, rice, tomatoes, tomato paste, chutney, and cloves. Simmer 1 hour. Add more broth if necessary. Puree in blender or food mill and serve with cream.

Optional addition: cooked chicken or shrimp, heated until warm.

## BUBBLE AND SQUEAK
*Phillip Harris, Three Horseshoes*

Fry chopped onion in hot drippings, then add a mixture of cooked potato and green vegetables (cabbage and sprouts are best). Cook until crispy brown.

*Mulligatawny Soup at the Three Horeshoes, Madingley.*

## CHICKEN SUPREME
## WALNUT TREE

*Frank Harding,*
*The Walnut Tree*

Take one chicken breast, cut a pocket in the flat side, and fill with a pâté made of chicken livers, brandy, and finely ground walnuts. Wrap carefully in bacon, cover with foil, and bake in a hot oven for 12–15 minutes. Serve with a creamy mushroom sauce.

## COUNTRY CHICKEN,
## HAM, AND MUSHROOM PIE

*Tony Saint,*
*The Bugle Horn*

Makes 2 oval 10-inch pies.

1½ pounds prepared puff pastry
¾ pint cooked white sauce
2½ ounces cooking sherry
1 ounce white wine (optional)
1½ pounds cooked chicken
1½ pounds cooked boiled ham
4 ounces cooked, sliced mushrooms
4 ounces frozen peas
2–4 ounces milk
Salt and freshly ground black pepper
Egg and milk pastry wash

Dice the cooked chicken and ham into ¾-inch chunks and place in a mixing bowl together with the peas (still frozen) and the cooked mushrooms. Heat the prepared white sauce in a pan, stirring continuously to avoid sticking. Add the sherry, wine, and sufficient milk to correct to a creamy consistency. Season to taste and pour over the contents in the mixing bowl. Divide between two pie dishes. Roll out the puff pastry on a floured board and cover and decorate the two pies. Brush with the egg wash and bake in a hot oven for 10 minutes.

Not all pubs serve meals. Snacks of some variety are usually available, but these can be a gamble in an unknown pub. Richard Boston describes pre-1970 pub food as "rarely going beyond crisps, pickled eggs, and sandwiches which were bought second-hand from British Railways." Indigestible presliced bread and sausages of questionable heritage are still served with a straight face in some pubs. And microwave ovens and returnable earthenware dishes with frozen contents make it possible, in some pubs, for a customer to order "lasagne" and "moussaka" and receive identical rations of wilted noodles and hamburger. But a pub with good food will always have the

appropriate reputation. A little local research can turn up wonderful homemade salads, pastries, and surprising specialties.

A pub and a restaurant are two different things, and any

publican or restaurateur will agree. The distinction is difficult to define, but easy to feel. In recent years, many pubs have expanded their food service and offer complete meals in restaurant surroundings, but the

heart of a pub will always be the bar.

The welcoming atmosphere of a good pub is a combination of many things—the character of the publican, the regulars, the conversation, the games, the general level of sound or silence, and the layout. The thing one encounters first in a pub (and almost always last in a restaurant) is the bar. It is the magnetism of this single fixture that provides the focal point for the pub, and a restaurant-addition, no matter how elegant or profitable or thoughtfully designed, is an addition nonetheless.

The White Hart, in Flitton, is a country pub displaying an impressive fish menu that leaves many restaurant *cartes* in the fast-food category. Somerset Moore, ten-year chef and propri-

*Somerset Moore and his staff in the main dining room of the White Hart, Flitton.*

etor, thinks of the White Hart as somehow more than a pub.

"The joy of us running a pub *with* a restaurant is that people can have a look first. They can see whether they like the temperature of the water. In a restaurant, the only time you get to look at the menu is when you sit down . . . here, there's a menu on the bar and you can just have a look."

The White Hart, shadowed by the village church, has a garden for summer eating and its own small vineyard. It serves midday and evening meals to a capacity of fifty appreciative patrons. Mr. Moore trained at the famous Connaught Hotel in London and studied with Madame Prunier, whom he regards as a "a great influence in starting a career selling fish."

"I've always liked the combination of the country inn and good cooking. It seems like such a British thing to do."

When he began on his own in 1968, Mr. Moore found a trend away from classical or traditional dishes and toward what he calls the "Mackerel and Marmalade Brigade."

"It was a folksy sort of restaurant cooking—and that's the sort of bizarre combination that they'd come up with . . . a whole school of amateur cooks who thought anything could go with anything, deciding to open restaurants. They sprouted up all over England. I hope I've never been thought of as being from that school."

Trained classically, Mr. Moore has been trying to "steer a course through the run-of-the-mill food products available to the Briton." To this end, he has specialized in fish and game, areas he considers neglected— even though, he observes, "Britain has such wonderful fish."

His menu inclues thirty wines, four champagnes, and an amazingly varied offering of twenty-one fresh fish dishes, prepared with care in a well-organized kitchen about the size of a large broom closet.

A publican's style and grace are always reflected in the presentation of the food and the service one gets in his pub. The White Hart clearly displays Somerset Moore's belief that English people appreciate good food and drink and want "the surroundings in which they enjoy them to be as good, if not better than, their own homes."

## OYSTER AND GUINNESS PIE

*Somerset Moore, The White Hart*

1 pound fine, lean beefsteak, cubed
¼ pound ox kidneys (optional)
½ pint Guinness
1 large onion, chopped
2 bay leaves
A sprig of thyme
1 ounce flour
1 tablespoon tomato puree
10 oysters (Pacific)

Marinate (preferably overnight) the beef and kidney in the Guinness with half the chopped onion, the bay leaves, thyme, and the tomato puree. Sauté the remaining onion. Drain the meat mixture well and add to the onion. Seal briefly and sprinkle with the flour, stirring it in. Cook out the roux. Add the marinade. If necessary, adjust the consistency with beef stock or water. Simmer for 30–40 minutes, depending on the quality of meat. Allow to cool. The dish will improve if left for another night. Place in a pie dish and add the raw oysters. Cover with a short crust pastry, wash with egg, and bake in 225°F oven for no more than 25 minutes. The oysters will toughen if overcooked.

### SHORT CRUST PASTRY

8 ounces each flour, lard, and butter, rubbed in well

Bind together with 2 tablespoons water and a little salt.

## CHEESE CROUTE FLORENTINE

*Frank Harding,*
*The Walnut Tree*

Prepare a dough for puff pastry. Roll and cut into triangles about 10 inches on the longest side. On half of each triangle layer fresh chopped spinach and curd cheese, and fold over to form an envelope. Seal the edges and briefly deep-fry before baking to a golden brown. This double process prevents the pastry from drying out too much. Serve with a tangy dip. Suggested is a spicy tomato, garlic, wine, and herb dip.

"I think *nouvelle cuisine* will go out as quickly as it came in, but what will remain is the visual presentation. That's where *nouvelle cuisine* will, I think, stay with us for many, many years."

PHILLIP HARRIS, *Three Horseshoes*

*This dish is most likely of late Georgian/early Victorian origin, when meals involved many courses. This was one of the "savouries," or final elements in a meal, served after the dessert to cut the sweet taste before serving the port.*

ANGELS ON HORSEBACK    *Somerset Moore, The White Hart*

Wrap large fresh oysters in thin strips of bacon. Be certain to remove the rind from the bacon, as it will curl when it cooks and begin to push the oysters out. Secure with a toothpick and grill until the bacon is crisp. When the bacon is just crisp, the oysters will be warmed through perfectly—additional time will make the oysters tough. Serve on thin trimmed toast slices. Seasonings are unnecessary, since the bacon and oysters are so flavorful.

"It's a simple recipe, though somewhat fiddly. We have some women customers who buy our scotch eggs and take them home and tell their husbands they made them themselves."

DIANNE PERRIER, *The White Horse*

## LAMB CHOPS

Val Wells-West, Ye Olde Bell

For ten people.

20 lamb chops
4–6 medium onions, chopped
2 pounds fresh plum tomatoes, sliced
1 pound large mushrooms, sliced
Fresh garlic, minced
Dried rosemary
Salt and pepper

Lightly brown chops in oil. Place in large casserole with layers of chopped onion. Add tomatoes and mushrooms. Add garlic and rosemary and salt and pepper to taste.

Make a sauce of 2 tablespoons Bisto (gravy browning mix), 1 tablespoon flour, and 1 large tablespoon tomato puree. Add 12–16 ounces red wine, and blend in sufficient water to cover chops. Add bay leaves and cook for 1½ hours in a medium oven.

## SCOTCH EGGS

Diane Perrier, *The White Horse*

6 hardboiled eggs, chilled and shelled
1 pound ground sausage (or skinned link sausages, ground)
1 egg
½ cup milk
Bread crumbs
Salt and pepper
Rosemary

Divide the sausage into six portions, one per hardboiled egg. Form into pancake-shaped flats about ½ inch thick and wrap around the eggs, forming a continuous "blanket" by rolling the wrapped eggs on the counter. Beat together the egg and the milk. Dip eggs in the egg-milk mixture, then in the bread crumbs, back in the egg mixture, and so on, until a generous coating is formed. Deep fry in vegetable oil for 4 minutes.

"The earliest recorded use of the words Welsh Rabbit is 1725; Welsh *Rarebit* is a bit of false etymologizing first recorded sixty years later. Obviously, a cheese dish which is called Welsh Rabbit is a joke, like Bombay Duck (a fish), or a Birmingham screwdriver (a hammer)."

RICHARD BOSTON, *Beer and Skittles*

STAR SPECIAL  *Lesley Reynolds,*
(WELSH RABBIT)  *The Star*

2 slices of toast
English mustard
4 ounces strong cheddar, grated
1 medium egg

Lightly toast 2 slices of bread. Spread with English mustard. Add beaten egg to grated cheese and spread over toast. Grill until golden brown. Garnish with tomato slices, lettuce, and cucumber.

## EGG BAKED WITH FINNAN HADDIE AND CREAM

*Somerset Moore, The White Hart*

This dish is as simple as it looks . . . a variation of Haddock Monte Carlo, a classic dish, good for supper or breakfast.

If finnan haddock is unavailable, any "cold-smoked" fish (especially cod) will do. Avoid "hot-smoked" fish, which is smoked longer and is rather hard.

Break about 1½ cups of the fish into 1-inch chunks and place in a dish. Pour cream over the top, break an egg into it, and bake in a medium oven until golden. Salt and pepper and serve with a sprig of parsley. Be careful of highly salted fish when adding salt.

"We call ourselves an inn—that doesn't have rooms. Basically we're here for the traveler to have something to eat and drink... whether it be a pint of beer and a sandwich, or something rather nice."
PHILLIP HARRIS, *Three Horseshoes*

# Bibliography

Beeton, Isabella. *Mrs. Beeton's Cookery for All.* London: Pan, 1982.

Boston, Richard. *Beer and Skittles.* Glasgow: Collins & Sons, 1976.

Brown, Derek. *Darts.* East Ardsley: EP Publishing, Ltd., 1978.

Burke, Thomas. *English Inns.* London: Collins, 1944.

David, Elizabeth. *Spices, Salt and Aromatics in the English Kitchen.* Harmondsworth: Penguin, 1970.

Finn, Timothy. "Pub Games," *Good Beer Guide.* St. Albans: CAMRA, 1981.

Greenhalgh, Jenny. "The Licensee and His Pub," *Time Gentlemen Please.* London: Save Britain's Heritage/CAMRA, 1983.

Hutt, Christopher. *The Death of the English Pub.* London: Arrow Books, 1973.

Jackson, Michael. *The World Guide to Beer.* London: Mitchell Beazley, 1977.

Keverne, Richard. *Tales of Old Inns.* London: Collins, 1939.

Manasian, David. "The Real Beer Battle," *Management Today* (October 1979), pp. 80–85, 165 ff.

Protz, Roger. *Pulling a Fast One.* London: Pluto Press, 1978.

Roney, Egon. *Pub Guide.* British Tourist Authority, 1976.

Sheppard, Francis. *Brakspear's Brewery.* Henley-on-Thames: Brakspear & Sons, Ltd., 1979.

Smith, Michael. *Fine English Cookery.* London: Faber and Faber, 1973.

Young, Jimmy. *A Short History of Ale.* London: David & Charles, 1979.